WAYS TO TRANSFORM JOB INTO CAREER WITHIN 30 DAYS

&

IMPORTANT OF CAREER IN HUMAN LIFE

Alabs opan

Copyright©

All right reserved no copy of this publication may be reproduced ,distributed or transmitted in any form or by any means including photocopying, recording or other electronic or mechanical method, without the prior written permission of the publisher except in the case of brief quotation embodied in the critical review and certain other non-commercial uses permitted by copyright law.

copyright © Alabs opans,2022.

Table of contents

Introduction

Chapter 1

Chapter 2

CHAPTER 3

Chapter 4

Summary

Introduction

This manual is one of the books that was developed by me.

This manual is designed for people who are ready and really in need of a job.

The manual provides theoretical exposures needed in providing a strong foundation for the aspect of job and career.

This book provides a typical area of life skills, money management, and employability.

This book presents a different chapter in a simple way to enable people to acquire jobs needed and career.

Chapter 1

A job

A job is what?
"JOB" stands for "Joining Others' Business" in its complete form. Job, meanwhile, is not an acronym. The term "job" refers to labour or a task. In society, a person's function is defined by their employment. A job is, more particularly, a regular task that is often performed in return for cash. Many individuals have many occupations, including those of employee, housewife, and parent. A

person may begin a job by hiring himself. Some occupations are legitimate, while others are not. Criminals who work illegally are still subject to punishment, even if they are employed.

The value of a job

A job can help you feel more purposeful because it gives you goals to strive for every day and a source of income to help you get by. Even if you decide to change occupations later in life, it may help you develop the knowledge and expertise you'll need for your whole career. Having a job may be important for the following additional reasons:

By engaging with customers, clients, or colleagues, socialisation may help you learn more about the world and make you feel more a part of it.

Fulfilment: With the job you're currently holding, you can feel as if you've accomplished a goal in your professional or personal life.

Income: By giving you the ability to pay for the basics, a job may provide you with the resources you need to be financially secure both now and in the future.

A job provides the chance to develop new abilities, including organising, public speaking, and customer service.

Wellness: Some occupations provide us with the chance to move throughout the day, which may improve our general health.

Chapter 2

kinds of work.

Thinkers
Contractors
Improversa
Producers

Are you continuously considering methods to make your firm better as a leader in your industry? Do you find it difficult to strike a balance when employing new staff between choosing those who can uphold the status quo and choosing those who can introduce the innovations you need to be competitive?

For all phases of the business cycle, from invention and design to manufacturing and marketing, successful organizations need a diverse team of employees in many job categories.

Thinking generates an idea.
Builders make the concept a reality.
Enhancements make it better.
In order to supply products and services to clients, producers do the task repeatably.

A job may be transitory (for instance, odd hourly employment) or last a lifetime (for example, judges). Jobs may be divided into full-or part-time, full-or part-week categories. They may be categorized as being contract-based, irregular, seasonal, self-employed, or transitory. Employees who have worked for a city, the military forces, industry, the police, or other services for a certain amount of time get smaller, ongoing payments known as "work compensation" from some government entities.

Alternative words for job activity include appointment, assignment, business, career, office, position, post, circumstance, spot, stint, task, and trade work.

The best way to tell whether your work is unhealthy is

How can you know whether the job you have is good for you?
Asking yourself how frequently you feel content at work will help you decide whether your present job is the right one for you. Using this method, you may monitor your feelings about your employment and determine if they are evolving. It could be time to explore other alternatives if you discover that there is no advancement at work. Other indicators that a job may not be healthy include poor cooperation; a culture where you don't feel respected or appreciated; excessive hours without overtime

compensation; and insufficient vacation time.

Ensure that the job is something you are enthusiastic about, if possible. You may also wish to consider these questions for yourself:

Do you look forward to coming to work each day?
Do you feel satisfied with your work?
When should a modification be made?
Do you have any complaints about your job?
Are you earning enough money in this job?
Do you need to pursue more schooling in order to advance?

Is this position suitable for you and your family?

CHAPTER 3

Career

What is it?

A person's "career" refers to a person's path through education, employment, and other facets of life. "Careers" may mean a variety of things. It may be seen from a variety of angles. A long-term job or profession is referred to as a "career."

It is a time frame spent working or practising a career. It may refer to a linear development that involves advancement or upward movement in common use.

For instance, he is progressing in his profession.

According to this definition, someone is only following a profession if they show consistent or quick growth in their position, wealth, or other indicators.

People who have not achieved progress or other noteworthy accomplishments do not actually have a career.
For instance, physicians and attorneys, for instance, are seen as having careers, while clerks and

mechanical workers are not. This definition implies that in order for one's job activities to be considered a career, one must attain a certain vocation or social standing.

"Career importance in human existence
Making a career plan is vital since it offers you much-needed direction and clarifies where you envision yourself in the future. It helps you become aware of your strengths and limitations, as well as the abilities and information needed to achieve your objectives in the future.

Our lives are mostly devoted to pursuing our professional ambitions, so it is crucial to ensure that the necessary steps were taken and the appropriate preparation was done in your formative years. Very few people are fortunate enough to be born with a clear mind, who know what they want to achieve, and who know where they envision themselves in the future. However, the bulk of us are unsure of what we want out of life, making planning crucial. Planning your career will give your life and career meaning and purpose.

Courses of work

Career pathways come in a variety of skill-based occupations. These include more physically demanding skills like labour, welding, plumbing, and mechanics.

Careers that are skill-related tend to be extremely hands-on, provide a service or tangible product, and are often compensated hourly. They need some talent and may be compensated as freelance work or on a job-by-job basis for odd tasks. Examples comprise:

Chef Sportsmen

Repair personnel
Plumbers, mechanics, or gardeners
Performers and artists who work in construction

Business or entrepreneurship: A business gives value to the consumer by engaging in trade or the sale of a novel item or service.

Therefore, if you want to follow this route, you will need funding as well as the ability to produce a product or service in order to launch your firm. Additionally, you will need a broad range of abilities, such as the ability to build a customer or supply chain or to hire the varied individuals who will make up your team. Many occupations or career paths need both ability and knowledge.

For instance, it is debatable whether coding is a skill-based or knowledge-based professional path. However, generally speaking, I would classify positions requiring physical work as skill-oriented employment, whereas the rest are knowledge-oriented ones. Even more practical professions like plumbing and welding still need some expertise. Here are some instances of occupations that roughly equally combine the use of knowledge and talents.

Independent Freelancers: Offering a service or a talent for sale is another kind of company. You already possess a foundational set of abilities or expertise in this, but you gain independence and market it as a freelancer. You are just a freelancer if you are not employed by a corporation. Chartered accountants, photographers, web developers, and painters are examples of this. In essence, everyone who is self-employed and unattached to an organisation is considered a freelancer.

Objectives of Career Development Systems

The main objective of designing a career development system is to foster better communication within the organization as a whole. It promotes communication at all levels of organizations for example manager and employee and managers and top management. Proper communication is the lifeblood of any organization and helps in solving several big issues.

Assisting with Career Decisions: A career development system provides employees as well as managers with helpful assistance with career decisions. They get an opportunity to assess their skills and competencies and know their goals and future aspirations. It helps them give a direction so that they can focus on achieving their long term career goals.

Better Use of Employee Skills: A career development system helps organization make better use of employee skills. Since managers know their skills and competencies and therefore, can put them at a job where they will be able to produce maximum output.

Setting Realistic Goals: Setting realistic goals and expectations is another main objective of a career development system. It helps both employees and organization to understand what is feasible for them and how they can achieve their goals.
Creating a Pool of Talented Employees: Creating a pool of talented employees is the main objective of organizations. After all, they need to meet their staffing needs in present and future and a career development system helps them fulfill their requirements.
Enhancing the Career Satisfaction: Organizations especially design career development systems for enhancing the career satisfaction of

their employees. Since they have to retain their valuable assets and prepare them for top notch positions in future, they need to understand their career requirements and expectations from their organization. Feedback: Giving feedback on every step is also required within an organization to measure the success rate of a specific policy implemented and initiatives taken by the organization. In addition to this, it also helps managers to give feedback for employees' performance so that they can understand what is expected of them.

A career development system can be very effective in creating a supportive culture in the organization and help employees grow and utilize their skills to achieve their desires and aspirations related to their career. Both organization and employees can meet their goals simultaneously.

10 tips for balancing work and family time

If you're finding it difficult to balance your career and family life, you're not alone. According to a 2015 survey, only 34% of full-time employees in the United States strongly believe they have a good work/life balance. While, for most of us, our career plays an essential role in our everyday life – there are some easy-to-implement ways to get better at balancing our work life alongside our family time.

1. Reduce your stress levels
Countless studies have explored the connection between stress and illness. One such study, carried out over five years in Belgium, concluded that high strain work environments combined with a lack of social support are "predictive of sick leave" within Belgium's workforce. With this in mind, reducing stress should be a no-brainer to anyone who's hoping to get the most out of their work-life and family time. The good news is, there are plenty of simple yet effective ways to relieve stress. Some

evidence-based techniques that you can apply to your everyday life include breathing exercises, meditation, cognitive behavioral therapy, and mindfulness exercises – to name a few.

2. Discuss workplace flexibility with your employer

If your current work structure is making it difficult to achieve work/life balance, consider approaching the topic with your employer. Workplace flexibility can make it much easier to juggle the demands of your personal life and professional obligations. Flexible working hours and having the option to work from home (where feasible) can help to make family commitments much more manageable. Chances are, you'll also experience a deeper sense of job satisfaction in the process.

3. Create a plan
If your weeks tend to lack structure and allocated family time, it might be time to draw up a plan. Map out what your weeks currently tend to look like: what isn't working? What aspects would you like to continue with? What parts of your week are compulsory? Once you've figured these things out, create a family calendar that allows you to move through your week at a slower pace –

allowing more time for the things that matter to you.

4. Focus on family-friendly workouts
"How do you workout when you have kids?" is a frequently searched question on Google. The answer? Incorporate exercise into your family time. A 2014 study found that there is a direct link between the physical activity levels of a mother and her children – which offers all the more inspiration to develop a family exercise routine. Choose activities that will allow you and your kids to workout while having fun. This could be a backyard soccer game, a family bike ride, indoor rock climbing, or

even just putting on some music and dancing around the house.

Prioritize and delegate

The reality is that many of us simply have too many things on our to-do lists. Rather than losing sleep, focus on your priorities. What are the things that simply must be on your calendar this week? List them in order of priority and check them off accordingly. Is there anything on your list that can be removed or postponed? At work, are you able to delegate any of your tasks? At home, can you lighten the house cleaning load by spreading it out amongst your family members – leaving more room for quality family time? This process of prioritizing and delegating can help to pave the way to achieving a better work/life balance.

6. Seek out support
If you've looked at your priorities, planned out a calendar, and have delegated certain tasks – yet still find that you're struggling to find a healthy balance between your work and family life – it might be time to seek support. Depending on your circumstances, this may mean: looking at childcare options, speaking to your siblings about supporting you in providing care to elderly parents, or perhaps hiring a cleaner to help you around the house. Go back to your calendar and see what tasks can be outsourced.

7. Schedule in phone calls

When you're balancing work, sleep, raising children, going to the gym, and spending time with your partner – it's understandable that other relationships might start to fall through the cracks. Particularly as many of us are balancing work and family during COVID-19 social distancing, it is so important to maintain these relationships. A simple way to keep in touch is to set a reminder on your phone to call your parents, grandparents, relatives, or friends. Over the years, researchers have found a clear link between the quality of our relationships and quality of life – so it's worth investing your time in that daily phone call.

8. Take a technology break
While technology plays an important role in providing work flexibility, constantly having your emails in the palm of your hand can be detrimental to a good work/life balance. It's advisable to set specific times during the day where you can put your technology away and simply enjoy being present with your family or friends. According to an article by Sonoma State University Professor of Psychology Mary Gomes, the benefits of taking a break from technology include: increased present-moment awareness, improved sleep, deeper human connections, and improved

productivity – all things that support work/life balance!

9. Develop a daily routine
Creating an everyday routine for yourself is almost as important as creating a daily routine for your kids. A daily routine can help you to develop a practice of taking some time for your wellbeing, a way to ease in and out of your work day, and can help to develop pockets of daily family time. These daily habits can be as simple as beginning your day with a health supplement, aiming to consistently start and finish work at set times, and eating dinner together as a family. It all starts with positive, achievable habits.

10. Take care of your mitochondria
Of course, achieving your career and family goals ultimately comes down to taking care of your health and energy levels. To do this, it's important to look after your body's mitochondria: the power banks that generate the energy and health your cells need for your body to function effectively. An easy way to support the health of your mitochondria is to take MitoQ – our world-first cellular optimizer designed to support mitochondrial health. If you'd like to learn more about how MitoQ can support your daily wellbeing and energy needs.

Chapter 4

How to Advance Your Career in One Month

-Plan out your search period.

You must dedicate 30 minutes a day to your job search if you want to get employment in 30 days. Nobody wants to spend a whole day revising their résumé. Be reasonable and finish a few things each day.

-Be aware of your goals:

Consider these important questions while you do your job search: What about your present employment don't you like? What makes you want to switch jobs? At this point, you should pause and give your values, requirements, and ideal workplace a lot of thought. Don't forget to take these factors into account, as well as your ideal income and other factors.

-Highlight your abilities.

Make a list of the abilities and traits that make you stand out from the competition. "What distinguishes you as special?" Identify your key abilities since you will need them in the next phase.

-Prepare your marketing materials by:

Your cover letter, LinkedIn profile, and CV are all marketing materials used to offer your service or product—you! Côté perceives things in this way. She says, "These instruments need to show us how this individual left their stamp." This is your opportunity to highlight your greatest successes from each position you've had.

-Develop a search plan:

It's time to focus on your job search now that you've established your objectives for the search, determined the qualifications that employers value in candidates, and refined your marketing materials. To put it another way, focus on the industries in which you'd want to work. For example, would you rather work for a small, medium, or big company? Which sector, the public or the private,

-Continue to be active online.

Make a profile on LinkedIn, the biggest professional network in the world, if you haven't already. Every jobseeker must take this step since there are 12 million Canadians on LinkedIn, including employers, headhunters, and human resource specialists.

-Make use of nearby assets and your own network.

People often overlook their local job centers and networking groups. However, these organizations offer the tools necessary to help you with your job hunt. This also holds true for your own social network. Conduct a covert survey of those around you, find individuals who work in the target industry you've picked, and make contact with top managers who are employed there. A lot of occupations don't have advertisements, so you have to be creative, as Côté tells us.

-Get ready for the interview:

Study the company, its major initiatives, and the individual you're meeting with. A lot of businesses also like it when applicants ask questions at the conclusion of the interview, since it shows genuine interest and purpose.

-Continue:

They often say they'll get back to you "soon" after the interview. This kind of evasiveness shouldn't deter you from expressing your interest again and following up with the interviewer. Tell them you enjoyed meeting with them and that you're looking forward to hearing from them.

-Continue searching

Finally, I caution that these measures may not be successful the first time. "You have to keep looking; don't spend all your efforts on a single job," the saying goes while looking for a job. Your efforts will eventually be acknowledged!

The importance of a career and a job in society
Why is labor so crucial to society?

A lengthy historical process led to the position of labor in modern cultures. It is essential for increasing people's feelings of usefulness and belonging, as well as for supplying resources. Work also plays a key part in a number of other areas, such as its function as a socializing mechanism, a venue for social interactions, and a source of personal identities. Work may thus be considered as the foundation of social organization and, to a significant degree, as a key pillar of personal existential organization. It is a crucial component of many aspects of social integration, including relationships, housing, and health. Thus, the need for Work

Integration Programs (WIP) designed to help disadvantaged populations.

Let's sum up the significance of employment for both individuals and society:

Individuals' daily routines, levels of activity, physical and mental well-being, self-confidence and self-esteem, and a sense of self-worth provided by the feeling of contributing to society or the common good are all influenced by their employment, which is a key factor in structuring their personal and social identity, family and social ties, means of generating income, and access to a variety of essential and non-essential goods, services, and activities.

Work is crucial for societies because it increases civic engagement, fosters community cohesion and safety, reduces public spending on a variety of welfare benefits (provided, of course, that work is done in a job that pays a decent wage), fosters social and economic development, and organizes macro social life.

Wins take on more significance when success in these aspects is threatened. Wins become even more important when macro-and micro-structural issues prevent work from playing its beneficial function in society. These should be given considerable thought.

As jobs become more precarious and subject to sudden change or elimination, people feel less commitment to and loyalty to both their jobs and one another (see: Public Policy).
Microstructural conditions: integration and work are not the same thing. In fact, low-status, low-paying, risky, unstable employment pushes people to the outside of society. Nevertheless, despite the present circumstances, employment still plays a crucial role in your life.

Interpersonal skill Develop your social skills to improve how you interact with others. Be warm and kind to friends in your network, and genuinely offer to help others when you're able. You can also be someone your colleagues come to confide in if they feel like they can trust you, which can help build your professional relationships. People love to share **ideas and opportunities with those closest to them.**

Communication

Your ability to communicate can determine how fast you move up in your career. Learning to communicate your ideas clearly in several ways is essential, especially for leadership positions. Develop and improve your written and verbal communication skills, as well as your ability to listen actively and be attentive to nonverbal cues. Taking a public speaking course can also be an asset, as professionals in senior roles typically speak to large groups of people or present high-level ideas to an audience.

Leadership

Your ability to lead a group is one of the most critical skills necessary to advance your career. As you develop professionally, you benefit from great managerial skills. To become an excellent leader, consider enrolling in leadership courses where you can build your confidence. Then volunteer to manage a team within or outside your company to apply your new leadership knowledge and skills.

Organisation

An organized leader helps a project progress within budget and on time. Employers are typically more encouraged to promote an employee who can achieve definite business goals by setting priorities, organizing workflow, and assigning tasks to team members. Developing your organizational skills can make it easier for you to complete your personal tasks more efficiently.

Skills to advance a career

1. Decide your career path

Career advancement can be in your current occupation or a different one. Although changing career paths may extend the time you take to make significant progression, it's important you advance in an occupation you enjoy. Once you decide on a profession you're passionate about, focus on acquiring all the education, skills, and experience, and build your professional network in the industry. This can help you progress to the top of your chosen career faster.

2. Set specific goals with deadlines

Define the specific position you want to reach in your career, and set medium and long-term goals to help you achieve them. Be clear on all the intermediate positions you must pass through to reach the top of your career and the time frame for each position. Create a list of short-term goals and actions you can take to reach them. For instance, if your long-term goal is to become the manager in your firm, your short-term goals could contain all the steps you need to take, skills to gain, and educational qualifications to obtain.

3.Consider creating SMART goals and writing them down. This is a helpful framework for setting specific, measurable, achievable, relevant, and time-based personal and professional goals. This method can help you define exactly what you want to do, when you want to achieve it, and how you plan to do so. You can then reference your goals regularly and assess your progress.

4.Monitor and track your progress
To find out if you're progressing in your career, develop a system to

monitor and track your progress consistently. Identify your strengths and weaknesses and seek help from your peers who have the same motivations as you. You can help hold each other accountable and encourage each other to succeed. Ensure you're taking the steps you planned and reaching those milestones that are critical to advancing in your career.

5. Share your career plans with a trusted friend or mentor and seek their feedback. Form a group of friends to help one another keep track of career progress. Develop a habit of regularly checking and reassessing your goals and performance so you can quickly identify when you need to make adjustments.

6. Join and grow your network
In your organization, find colleagues who are career-driven like you and spend time with them. Select your network of friends with only people you trust,

as they can exchange valuable ideas and information with you. This helps you to stay on top of industry events and trends that can assist you in advancing in your career.

Consider joining your professional association and become an active member. Go for meetings and take part so industry leaders with influence in your field can notice you and help. Actively seek and inquire about networking events in your field because they provide advancement opportunities to meet potential future employers who may be interested in hiring you.

7. Find a mentor

A mentor is someone who has a profound knowledge about your field and has successfully passed through all the stages of advancement in your career. It is preferable to select a mentor in your industry, but not compulsory. Choose a mentor who listens to you and provides the essential advice for you to advance your career.

A good mentor guides you and offers to help you when you feel stuck. To benefit from mentorship, be open with your mentor and share all the details that can help your mentor provide the necessary guidance. To find a mentor, create a checklist of qualities your ideal mentor may have and then seek one by networking both inside and outside your organization.

8.Interpersonal skills
Develop your social skills to improve how you interact with others. Be warm and kind to friends in your network, and genuinely offer to help others when you're able. You can also be someone your colleagues come to confide in if they feel like they can trust you, which can help build your professional relationships. People love to share ideas and opportunities with those closest to them.

9. Communication

Your ability to communicate can determine how fast you move up in your career. Learning to communicate your ideas clearly in several ways is essential, especially for leadership positions. Develop and improve your written and verbal communication skills, as well as your ability to listen actively and be attentive to nonverbal cues. Taking a public speaking course can also be an asset, as professionals in senior roles typically speak to large groups of people or present high-level ideas to an audience.

10 Leadership

Your ability to lead a group is one of the most critical skills necessary to advance your career. As you develop professionally, you benefit from great managerial skills. To become an excellent leader, consider enrolling in leadership courses where you can build your confidence. Then volunteer to manage a team within or outside your company to apply your new leadership knowledge and skills.

Organization

An organized leader helps a project progress within budget and on time. Employers are typically more encouraged to promote an employee who can achieve definite business goals by setting priorities, organizing workflow, and assigning tasks to team members. Developing your organizational skills can make it easier for you to complete your personal tasks more efficiently.

Curiosity
Asking questions is an important learning process when you're with your mentor, or while observing industry leaders you admire. Ask specific and appropriate questions

that show your willingness to grow. Prepare questions ahead of time so you can get answers to questions that may help you advance your career.

Summary

Don't simply concentrate on the what, such as what you did in the past and what you do today, while introducing yourself to new coworkers. Include why instead. Discuss your reasons for choosing this position as well as your love for the organisation or industry. This will naturally increase the interest level of introductions and create a favourable and long-lasting impression on those who hear them.
What do people anticipate from you? Meetings with a number of important partners often take place within the first few weeks on the job. What do

you anticipate from me? This is a crucial question to ask during these encounters.

This will enable you to establish a tight bond with each partner and clarify how you can live up to expectations.

Know the metrics used to evaluate your management.

Being effective in any profession requires knowing how to handle your management. And in order to accomplish this properly, you must comprehend the standards by which they will be judged.

There could be one standard to which they are held. Or maybe it has more to do with how their team members feel about their team's performance or

cooperation within. Whatever it may be, your chances of building a better connection with your boss will significantly rise if you can figure out what matters to them the most.
Make several inquiries.

Lots of inquiries Ask for an inquiry if you are uncertain.

Most people will value this since it demonstrates your genuine desire to learn. Furthermore, you must be eager to learn because business is frequently complex, and you must grasp it quickly.

Therefore, if you're unsure, ask a question. Compared to attempting to figure things out on your own, it will bring you up to speed far more quickly.

Spend some time studying the organizational structure of your larger team. You'll be able to collaborate with the right individuals since you'll be familiar with their names, their

responsibilities, and their backgrounds.
Make it up and practice your pitch. In your first two weeks, you'll have a number of new encounters. Within that time frame, develop and fine-tune your elevator pitch about who you are and what you do. Keep in mind the advice from the first item on this list, and keep it in mind. Therefore, you should be able to briefly describe what you accomplished within the first month. However, if you can, include a sentence explaining why you love your work.

CONCLUSION

The paper revealed that most people refuse to make use of methods stated in this book because they believe that it takes time to apply to those methods listed which is not true. At the end of this book a solution was produced in order to secure a job & career faster.

RECOMMENDATION

The paper recommends that the teachers should always show students the moral method that peoples need to secure job & career faster during the school days, In order not to affect them in future.